JAMES BUCHANAN

PRESIDENTIAL ✦ LEADERS

JAMES BUCHANAN

SANDY DONOVAN

⌐ LERNER PUBLICATIONS COMPANY / MINNEAPOLIS

Lerner Publications Company
A division of Lerner Publishing Group
241 First Avenue North
Minneapolis, MN 55401 U.S.A.

Website address: www.lernerbooks.com

Library of Congress Cataloging-in-Publication Data

Donovan, Sandra, 1967–
    James Buchanan / by Sandy Donovan.
        p.   cm. — (Presidential leaders)
    Includes bibliographical references and index.
    ISBN: 0–8225–1399–4 (lib. bdg. : alk. paper)
    1. Buchanan, James, 1791–1868—Juvenile literature. 2. Presidents—United States—Biography—Juvenile literature. I. Title. II. Series.
    E437.D66 2005
    973.6'8'092—dc22   2004017902
    921 Buchanan, James

Manufactured in the United States of America
1 2 3 4 5 6 – JR – 10 09 08 07 06 05

CONTENTS

———————— ✧ ————————

Buchanan (tipping his top hat) *rides with Abraham Lincoln on the way to Lincoln's swearing-in ceremony in March 1861.*

INTRODUCTION

A NATION DIVIDED

My dear sir, if you are as happy in entering
the White House as I shall feel on returning
[home], you are a happy man indeed.
—James Buchanan to Abraham Lincoln

President James Buchanan woke up in the White House on March 4, 1861, with a great sense of relief. Later that day, Abraham Lincoln would be sworn in as president. Buchanan would head home to Pennsylvania—leaving his troubles behind. And his troubles were great. After years of bitterness between the North and the South, the United States stood on the brink of civil war. Four years earlier, Buchanan had been elected president with the promise of keeping the Union (United States) together. By early 1861, there seemed little chance of avoiding bloodshed. The outgoing president was happy he would not be presiding over a nation at war.

Outside the White House, the day was cloudy and windy. Inside, Buchanan took a final walk around his home of the past four years, saying good-bye to staff and friends. Just after noon, he climbed into an open carriage that would take him down Pennsylvania Avenue to Willard's Hotel, where Lincoln was staying. At the hotel, Lincoln climbed into the carriage, wearing a top hat and black coat. As the carriage made its way to the U.S. Capitol for the inauguration (swearing-in) ceremony, thousands of well-wishers lined the streets.

The celebratory feeling masked the fear and uncertainty filling the country. Although war had not yet been declared, seven southern states—angry with the federal government over the issue of slavery—had already left the Union. Southern troops had fired on a northern ship in South Carolina. Many threats had been made to assassinate Lincoln, the new, pro-northern president. The streets of Washington, D.C., the nation's capital, were lined with U.S. cavalry troops, rifles drawn.

If Buchanan and Lincoln were nervous about the threats of violence, neither man displayed fear during the carriage ride. Observers said that the two chatted in a friendly manner for most of the ride. Upon arriving at the Capitol, Buchanan turned to Lincoln and said he hoped Lincoln was as happy to be entering the White House as Buchanan was to be leaving it. To this, Lincoln replied, "I cannot say that I shall enter it with much pleasure, but I assure you that I will do what I can to maintain the high standards set by my illustrious predecessors [earlier presidents]."

After nearly fifty years as a politician, James Buchanan was ready to return to private life. During his presidency, the Union had started to break apart. He felt he had done his best during the nation's crisis, acting as a buffer between the North and the South. Others were not so sure that Buchanan had done his best. Many accused him of failing to prevent the nation's bloodiest war. The truth is perhaps somewhere in between these two views.

CHAPTER ONE

IMMIGRANT'S SON

*I am not disposed to [criticize] you
for being ambitious.*

—James Buchanan's father to his son

Nine-year-old James Buchanan closed one eye and concentrated hard on the handwritten pages in front of him. He was perched on a stool behind the counter at his father's general store in Mercersburg, Pennsylvania. James's father had taught his son to be the store's record keeper. In this job, James wrote down the prices of everything that came into the store (how much the store paid for goods) and the prices of everything that went out (how much the customers paid). At the end of each month, he added up those amounts to see how much money the store had made. This work was difficult. For James, it was especially hard because he was extremely nearsighted in one eye, so he kept one eye closed for reading. But James loved his father, and he worked hard to impress him.

James's father, also named James, had moved to the United States from Ireland fourteen years earlier. He had come to rural Lancaster County, Pennsylvania, at the age of twenty-two to live with his uncle and seek his fortune. Soon he bought a small trading post, or store, and married Elizabeth Speer. The couple's first child died in infancy. But they then had James, in 1791, Jane in 1793, and Maria in 1795.

The Buchanans' trading post was located right next to a gap in the Allegheny Mountains of western Pennsylvania. Travelers from Philadelphia and Baltimore, going west to Pittsburgh or beyond, passed through this area, called

───────────────────── ✧ ─────────────────────

Americans who traveled westward in the late 1700s and 1800s had to leave behind friends and family they might never see again.

Cove Gap. The official road ended there, so travelers switched from wagons to horses to continue their journey. All this activity provided a steady stream of customers for the Buchanans' trading post. But Elizabeth Buchanan decided that a trading post was not the right environment for young children. Plenty of rough people passed through the gap, and the jumble of wagons and horses could be dangerous to people on foot.

So James Buchanan Sr. found a plot of land in the center of the small town of Mercersburg, about one mile north of Cove Gap. The family moved there in 1797, when young James was six years old. James Sr. built a two-story brick house, with a general store on the first floor and a

————————————— ✧ —————————————

The Buchanan family lived in this sturdy cabin in Cove Gap, Pennsylvania.

home upstairs for his growing family. Eventually, the Buchanans would have eleven children, although three died as babies. Until he was fourteen, James was the only boy in the family and the center of attention from his parents and his younger sisters.

LEARNING AT HOME

As a boy and the oldest child, James was expected to spend many hours a week helping out in the family store. He learned the value of hard work and thrift from his father, who had been an orphan in Ireland and was determined to make a better life for his family. James's father was stern, and he made James work hard. But he loved his son, and he wanted him to do well in life. He taught James to pay close attention to business and to remember details. James's mother was less strict. She did not have much education, but she loved to read. She inspired James with a love of books and learning.

James also learned a lot from the local farmers who came to his father's store. From behind the counter, young James heard these men discussing politics. He learned about the two prominent political parties of the day. The Federalist Party believed in a strong central U.S. government, strong banking and business sectors, and a government run by the upper classes. The Democratic-Republican Party favored a weak central government and strong state governments. It felt that all white men—rich and poor—should have a say in government. (At the time, many black Americans were slaves, and only white men were allowed to vote.) As a business owner, James's father supported the Federalists, although many farmers in the area were Democratic-Republicans.

Also at his father's store, James developed sympathy for the rural, farming lifestyle of his customers. These farmers were people who cherished family tradition and did not welcome change easily. They respected landownership more than money or other possessions. The rural lifestyle was very different from the fast-paced way of life found in the nation's big cities such as Philadelphia, Pennsylvania, and Boston, Massachusetts. There, commerce—buying and selling—was the foundation of society, and people had little patience for slower, traditional ways.

———————————————— ✧ ————————————————

Farmers work with oxen to clear away stones from a field.
James knew many farming families in Mercersburg.

By the early 1800s, Philadelphia was already a bustling city.

James learned arithmetic from his duties at the store. He also learned the importance of keeping track of details and using neat handwriting for record keeping. Although these lessons were valuable, James's father understood the importance of a formal education as well. So he sent James to study Greek and Latin with Dr. John King, a church pastor.

When James turned sixteen, Dr. King urged his father to send the boy to nearby Dickinson College. Although James's father needed his son's help at the store, he also knew that an advanced education would help James get ahead in the United States. Being an orphan, the elder James also knew what could happen to a family if a father died young. With six children at that point and another on the way, the elder James wanted to make sure his son could provide for his sisters if necessary. James's mother wanted her son to become a minister, but her husband insisted that their son prepare for a career as a lawyer. As a lawyer, his father reasoned, James would always be able to provide for his family.

So in 1807, young James traveled with his father to Carlisle, Pennsylvania, to attend Dickinson. Since James had already studied with Dr. King, he was able to skip his freshman and sophomore years of study. He joined the school as a junior.

A NOT-SO-SERIOUS STUDENT

At Dickinson, James joined forty-one other students. The students were all young white men, and all but two of them were from Pennsylvania. When James arrived, much of the college campus was under construction. As James later said, it was "in wretched condition." A new and elegant main college building had almost been completed just before James entered. But six weeks short of being finished, it had burned to the ground when someone carelessly left a bucket of hot ashes in the basement. A replacement building was under construction.

James studied Latin, Greek, literature, philosophy, history, mathematics, and geography at Dickinson. At first, he threw himself into his classes and spent all his free time studying. Soon, however, he realized that he was not making many friends by being such a serious student. As he later wrote, "to be a sober, plodding, industrious student was to incur the ridicule of the mass of students." In other

Dickinson College, early 1800s

words, studying was not making James very popular. Before long, James was paying less attention to his classes and more to his social life.

At home James had always been fairly spoiled by his parents and younger sisters. Away from home for the first time, he began acting like someone special at school too. Although he was capable of completing all his assignments, he often went to class without his homework. He began to talk back to his teachers. He spent more and more time in town, drinking and smoking cigars with his friends—two activities that were forbidden by the school. Despite this behavior, James was smart enough to earn passing grades, even without putting much effort into his classes.

In the summer of 1808, he returned home to Mercersburg and the attentions of his parents and sisters. He enjoyed his summer in his hometown, getting together with old friends and planning for his return to Dickinson for his senior year.

But one leisurely summer afternoon, his enjoyment was interrupted by a knock at his parents' front door. When his father answered the door, a messenger handed him a letter. James watched as his father tore open the letter, curious about the news. James continued to watch as his father's face turned red with anger. He thrust the letter at James and stormed out of the room. Stunned, James picked up the paper and read with disbelief that he was being thrown out of school. The college president wrote that James's disruptive behavior had gotten out of hand, and he would not be invited back to Dickinson in the fall. James could not believe his eyes. It was the first time he had been in real trouble in his life.

James could not face his father's anger, so he turned to his old teacher, Dr. King, for help. Dr. King was on the board of trustees (governing body) at Dickinson and had helped get James into the school in the first place. Buchanan later wrote about his discussion with Dr. King: "He gave me a gentle lecture. He then proposed to me that if I would pledge on my honor to him to behave better at college than I had done, he felt such confidence in me that he would pledge himself to [the college president] on my behalf, and he did not doubt that I would be permitted to return."

With Dr. King's help, James was allowed to return to Dickinson for his senior year. He made good on his promise to behave better. He excelled at his schoolwork. Some of his professors came to think of him as a conceited young man, who was mostly interested in impressing others with his intelligence. He finished his senior year in the summer of 1809 and graduated with honors.

Buchanan lived around the corner from the Lancaster courthouse (above) while he studied to become a lawyer.

CHAPTER TWO

LOVE AND POLITICS

He was cut out by nature for a great lawyer.
—a Lancaster judge, speaking of James Buchanan

After graduating from Dickinson, Buchanan moved to Lancaster, then Pennsylvania's capital, to study law. With a population of six thousand, Lancaster was the largest town in the United States not located on the Atlantic coast. As the state capital, Lancaster was home to a lot of lawyers who worked with state officials. For one year, Buchanan studied law with James Hopkins, a Lancaster lawyer with a good reputation throughout Pennsylvania. This arrangement, called a preceptorship, involved on-the-job training in law. Buchanan helped Hopkins with legal research and courtroom work. He lived in rented rooms at an inn that was located a block and a half from the courthouse and across the street from Hopkins's grand mansion.

Once Buchanan finished his preceptorship, he was ready to begin practicing law. He thought about practicing in

Lancaster, but Pennsylvania's capital was being moved to Harrisburg. Buchanan was afraid this switch would leave an overflow of lawyers in Lancaster, with not enough work to go around once the state government left.

Buchanan was interested in seeking adventure out west, in Kentucky. He had heard that this new frontier state was a good place for a young man to begin a career. Coincidentally, James's father owned about 3,600 acres of Kentucky land, but someone else also claimed ownership. The two men took the argument to court. Buchanan decided to head west and begin his law practice by defending his father's land claim. However, when he arrived in Elizabethtown, Kentucky, in 1812, he found the legal dispute to be far more complicated than he had imagined. He had the feeling that the case would drag on for many years. Realizing it would not be any easier to open a law office in Kentucky than in Pennsylvania, he returned to Lancaster.

For the next two years, Buchanan practiced law in Lancaster. His careful business habits and attention to detail earned him a reputation as a good lawyer. He attracted a lot of clients and began to make a lot of money. His name became well known around Lancaster.

He also became interested in politics. As his father had, he supported the Federalist Party, the party of big business and a strong federal government. In 1814 the local Federalist group asked Buchanan to run for state assemblyman. In this position, he would represent his town in the Pennsylvania legislature (lawmaking body). At the time, the Federalists were the minority party in Pennsylvania. That is, they had fewer elected officials in state government than the Democratic-Republicans had. But the Federalists had strong support in Lancaster. As the Federalist candidate for assemblyman from that town, Buchanan was assured a victory in the election.

Before the election took place, a larger event interrupted politics across the country. The War of 1812 (1812–1814), between the United States and the British, had been going on for two years. The war had begun over disputes about maritime (ocean) shipping. It became more intense when the British invaded Washington, D.C., in August 1814. British troops burned the White House and other government buildings.

───────────────── ◆ ─────────────────

In this War of 1812 battle, the USS Constitution captures the British HMS Guerrière.

British troops set fire to buildings in Washington, D.C.

The Federalists opposed the war because they thought it would destroy trade between the United States and Europe. As a Federalist, Buchanan also opposed the war, and he believed that the government of President James Madison—a Democratic-Republican—was doing a poor job of trying to end it. But as a political candidate, Buchanan needed to volunteer to fight. He wanted to show that he was willing to defend his country.

So in late August 1814, at the age of twenty-three, Buchanan joined about twenty other young men from Lancaster and rode his horse to Maryland. They volunteered for the U.S. Army and were assigned to help defend Baltimore, a town near Washington, D.C., from the British. U.S. forces repelled the British attack on Baltimore, but Buchanan saw no fighting during the event. He was soon on his way home.

FIRST POLITICAL POST

Buchanan arrived back in Lancaster about a month before the election. As expected, he easily won the race for assemblyman. He headed to Harrisburg in the fall of 1814. Harrisburg was then a sleepy town that had served as Pennsylvania's capital for two years. Buchanan rented rooms at the Golden Eagle Inn on Market Square. Across the square stood the county courthouse, which served as a temporary capitol while a new capitol building was under construction.

Buchanan took his seat in the state legislature. This governing body included one hundred assemblymen, like Buchanan, and thirty senators. Together, these men wrote, debated, and voted on proposed state laws, which were then submitted to the governor for approval.

Buchanan's first long speech before his fellow assemblymen dealt with increasing the size of the U.S. military. At first, the U.S. government had relied on volunteer soldiers to create its army. But Pennsylvania state senators had voted to begin drafting (selecting) young men from Pennsylvania to serve in the military, in case the state came under attack from the British.

Buchanan gave a speech in favor of continuing to use volunteers, arguing that a draft unfairly targeted poor people. He explained that the wealthy could send their sons to college, and college students were excluded from the draft. Therefore, most of the men drafted would be poor. He spoke passionately about defending poor citizens from the power of the rich. Many who heard the speech considered it to be brilliant. However, Buchanan's ideas went against many core Federalist beliefs, including the belief in a large army and navy. In fact, in his defense of the poor against the elite, Buchanan sounded more like a Democratic-Republican than a Federalist, and he angered many of the powerful people in his party.

Although he did not say so at the time, Buchanan was starting to move away from his Federalist views. But when he decided to run for a second term in the legislature, he knew he had to strengthen his support among the Lancaster Federalists who had elected him the first time. So on July 4, 1815, he delivered a fiery speech denouncing Democratic-Republican president James Madison. In the speech, Buchanan blamed the Democratic-Republicans for bringing the United States into an unnecessary war and

◇ ————————

Buchanan gave a speech condemning President James Madison (left) that helped him win reelection to the state legislature.

practically bankrupting the country. He also criticized the president for two recent acts: dismantling the country's central bank and ending national taxation. Buchanan's speech angered Democratic-Republican farmers from his home county of Lancaster. Still, many of the state's Democratic-Republicans were growing more and more unhappy with Madison, and they agreed with much of what Buchanan had to say about him.

Buchanan's Fourth of July speech helped him win reelection in the fall, and he served another year in Harrisburg. In 1816 he returned to Lancaster a much better known man than when he had left two years earlier. His name recognition helped him pick up his law practice and attract more clients. For the next few years, he took on more and more cases and built up his practice.

ROMANCE AND TRAGEDY

Back in Lancaster, Buchanan built up a strong professional reputation as a lawyer. He also earned a reputation as one of the town's most eligible bachelors. He was good-looking—tall and broad shouldered with wavy blond hair and blue eyes. And as a successful lawyer, he was invited to many society gatherings around town.

It was at one of these events, in 1818, that twenty-seven-year-old Buchanan met Ann Coleman. Ann was twenty-two years old and tall, with curly black hair and large, dark eyes. Many in Lancaster considered her beautiful. She was the daughter of Robert Coleman, one of the richest men in the United States, who had made a fortune in iron mining. Ann and James fell in love over the winter of 1818–1819. They spent their free time attending parties

*Sleigh rides were a fun and practical way to travel
during the snowy Pennsylvania winters.*

———————————————— ✧ ————————————————

and other social events. They took long sleigh rides through
the countryside and stopped for weekend visits at the
estates of other wealthy young people around Pennsylvania.

In the summer of 1819, James and Ann became
engaged. They looked forward to a large wedding. But not
everybody was happy about the union. Ann's parents did
not think Buchanan was good enough for her, and other
people in Lancaster began studying his every move, trying
to judge if he deserved to marry Ann Coleman. When, in
the fall of 1819, Buchanan had to spend more time on his
business and less time courting Ann, people gossiped that
he was more in love with Ann's fortune than with her. After
hearing more and more of this gossip, as well as her own
parents' objections to her marriage, Ann herself began
doubting Buchanan's feelings. She wrote him a letter, saying

she thought he cared more for money than for her. Buchanan was hurt by her accusations, but he did not know how to convince her otherwise.

Before Buchanan was able to clear things up with Ann, another misunderstanding occurred. Returning from an out-of-town business trip in early December 1819, he stopped to visit a few friends before visiting Ann. A pretty, young female relative happened to be visiting Buchanan's friends at the same time. Although the visit was completely innocent, local gossips talked about the two being a couple. The gossip convinced Ann that she had something to be jealous about, and in the heat of the moment, she wrote a letter to Buchanan, breaking their engagement. A few

———————— ✧
Ann Coleman (right) *accepted Buchanan's marriage proposal, but the two never married.*

days later, Ann left Lancaster for Philadelphia to visit her sister. Just one day after arriving, Ann became violently ill. Doctors were baffled by her sudden and mysterious illness. She died that night.

Early the next morning, a messenger arrived at Buchanan's door with the news of Ann's death. He was devastated. He immediately wrote to Ann's parents, expressing his sorrow and asking to attend the funeral. "I may sustain the shock of her death," he wrote, "but I feel that happiness has fled from me forever."

In their grief, Ann's parents blamed Buchanan for their daughter's death and refused to answer his letter. Others in Lancaster also believed Buchanan was responsible for her death. They assumed he had treated Ann so badly that she had become deathly ill—or even killed herself. As one resident wrote at the time: "It is now thought that this will lessen his [importance] in Lancaster as he is the whole conversation of the town." As a tribute to Ann, Buchanan vowed that he would never marry.

CHAPTER THREE

TO WASHINGTON: CONGRESSMAN BUCHANAN

*It ought to be a [rule] in politics . . . that an
officer of your Government shall be presumed
to have done his duty until the reverse
of the proposition is true.*
—Representative James Buchanan, speaking in
support of Secretary of War John C. Calhoun

After the tragedy of Ann's death and perhaps as a distraction
from his grief, Buchanan once again became involved in
politics. The Democratic-Republicans in Pennsylvania were
beginning to break into two factions, or groups. One group
supported the current Democratic-Republican governor,
and another joined with the Federalists to form the Federal-
Republicans. This new party wanted a strong candidate for
the House of Representatives, part of the U.S. Congress,
from the Lancaster district. Party leaders asked Buchanan
to run. Nationally, citizens were growing more and more

*This view of the capital in the early 1800s shows how Washington, D.C.,
looked when Buchanan first moved there to serve as a congressman.*

———————————————— ✧ ————————————————

dissatisfied with the government in Washington, D.C., and
the new Federal-Republicans appealed to voters.

Buchanan easily won the election in the fall of 1820.
He began preparing to move to Washington the following
year. His term as a congressman would begin in
December 1821. But in the meantime, more personal
tragedy struck. His father died unexpectedly in June of
1821. When Buchanan returned home for the funeral, he
found that his father had not left a will. Buchanan spent
the rest of his summer sorting out his father's affairs in a
way that would provide for his mother and his three
brothers and two sisters still living at home.

In November 1821, Buchanan left Lancaster by stage-
coach and headed for Washington, D.C. The national
capital, which had been burned by the British during the

War of 1812, had still not been completely rebuilt. When Buchanan arrived, he found many unfinished buildings and shabby houses. Pennsylvania Avenue, site of the Capitol and the White House, was a muddy mess of potholes. But Buchanan was eager to get to work. He quickly rented rooms at a boardinghouse where many other members of Congress lived.

Generally, new members of Congress spend their first few months learning their jobs, and they draw little attention to themselves. They vote on bills that come before their body—the House or the Senate—but they do not usually give long speeches. However, just a few weeks after Buchanan arrived in Washington, another congressman became ill. The congressman had been scheduled to give an important speech in support of John C. Calhoun, the

✧ ———

Buchanan's speech supporting John C. Calhoun (left), impressed other members of Congress.

secretary of war, and of a bill authorizing additional money for Calhoun's War Department.

Buchanan was known to be a powerful speaker, and he was friendly with the sick congressman, so Calhoun's friends asked Buchanan to make the speech. He considered it a great honor to be asked to speak, and he gave such an effective speech that the bill passed easily. Not only was Buchanan an excellent speechwriter and speaker, but he was loud enough to be heard by everyone in the House chamber—a feat not all representatives could accomplish. Suddenly, people in Washington were interested in the new representative from Pennsylvania.

Meanwhile, Buchanan's political feelings were still changing. As a Federal-Republican, Buchanan was aligned with the Federalist Party and was considered a Federalist in Congress. But though his party favored a strong national government, he found himself more and more believing in the rights of individual states.

JACKSONIAN DEMOCRACY

In 1822 Buchanan was elected to a second term in Congress and in 1824 to a third term. Around Washington, D.C., he was becoming more and more recognizable. At six feet, he was taller than many of his colleagues. He carried himself like a man of importance, with a straight back. Because he was nearsighted in one eye, he constantly turned his head to the side to see clearly. In conversations, this habit often gave listeners the impression that Buchanan was concentrating very hard on what they were saying. He gained a reputation as a serious man. He also made a point of enjoying the finer things in life, such as good food and fine wine. As one of the city's most eligible bachelors, he was rarely without a dinner invitation.

Buchanan took a keen interest in presidential politics during the presidential election of 1824. The Federalist Party was quickly losing power, and five Democratic-Republicans—John Quincy Adams, John C. Calhoun, Henry Clay, William H. Crawford, and Andrew Jackson—ran for president in that election. The contest came down to a race between Adams, the nation's secretary of state, and General Jackson, a war hero who had earned his reputation by fighting in the War of 1812 and by fighting Native Americans.

Buchanan opposed Adams and supported Jackson, who won the popular election—the vote by the people—by a landslide. But in the Electoral College—a system by which state electors (representatives) choose the president based only in part on the popular vote—no candidate received

Andrew Jackson (right) *was a war hero and a Democrat.*

the necessary majority. By law, the House of Representatives then chooses the president, and it elected Adams.

Although his candidate had lost the election, Buchanan continued to support Jackson and the party that came to be known as the Jacksonian Democrats (an offshoot of the Democratic-Republicans). In 1828, after being elected to Congress four times as a Federalist, Buchanan ran as a Democrat. Andrew Jackson again ran for president. Both Buchanan and Jackson easily won their elections that year. Three years later, as a thank-you for his support, President Jackson appointed Buchanan to be the U.S. minister, or ambassador, to Russia, an appointment that would last two years.

DIPLOMAT

Although the appointment as Russian minister was an honor, Buchanan was not excited by the prospect of moving so far away for two years. For one thing, he would miss the comforts of his own country. But even more importantly, he would miss being involved in national politics. In fact, he had had hopes of being named a vice-presidential candidate in the next election. The Russian appointment put that on hold, since he would be out of the country during the election. But Buchanan knew he needed to accept the post to maintain the support of Jackson and the current administration.

On January 12, 1832, the U.S. Senate voted unanimously to confirm Buchanan's appointment. Buchanan would not leave for Russia for a few months, but he got right to work learning French, the official language of the Russian government. He also began studying trade issues—

Buchanan spent a year and a half in Saint Petersburg,
where he served as the U.S. ambassador to Russia.

the ins and outs of shipping and commerce between Russia
and the United States. Improving trade relations between
the two countries would be the focus of his new job.

In the spring of 1832, Buchanan set out for Russia by
ship. After a two-week stop in Britain, he arrived in Saint
Petersburg, the Russian capital, in early June. At the time,
Saint Petersburg was one of the great cultural centers of
Europe. For business and government leaders, social life
revolved around grand invitation-only dinners and balls, as
well as visits to the theater and ballet. As a diplomat,
Buchanan was invited to many formal events at the court

Czar Nicholas I

——————— ✧ ———————

of Czar Nicholas I, Russia's leader. There, thanks to Buchanan's language studies, he was able to hold conversations in French.

Work was going well, but Buchanan was lonely in this stuffy atmosphere. He missed his own country. Upon arriving in Russia, he learned that his fellow U.S. diplomats in Saint Petersburg had not received news from the United States for more than a year. The Americans had no idea what was happening at home. As one of his first actions, Buchanan began a monthly mail service between Washington and Saint Petersburg.

He threw himself into his job of representing the interests of the United States in Russia. Within a few months, he had negotiated the first-ever trade treaty between the two countries. But Buchanan grew increasingly unhappy so far from home. At the same time, word came from the

United States that both his mother and his favorite brother George, had died. His brother Edward and his sister Harriet had both married during his absence. Buchanan was eager to return to his family.

Learning that Buchanan was unhappy, President Jackson sent word in the summer of 1833 that Buchanan could end his assignment early. In August he happily left Saint Petersburg. But before sailing for home, he made several official stops in European cities. He sailed first for Hamburg, Germany, and from there traveled to Paris, France, and London, England. In these two capital cities, he met many influential political leaders as well as nobility (aristocrats such as princes and dukes) from across Europe. He saw how Europeans felt about the United States, and he began to develop his own ideas on foreign policy.

——————————————— ✧ ———————————————

Buchanan visited Paris (below)*, the capital of France, on his way home from Russia.*

Buchanan wrote home to President Jackson: "Dear General . . . Our position in the world is now one of importance. The Allied powers [Russia, Prussia, and Austria] entertain no jealousy toward us." But after meeting with several French and British leaders, he developed a distrust of France and Great Britain. He felt that those nations were competitive with and jealous of the United States and its growing importance in world affairs.

Although Buchanan had not been excited about his appointment to Russia, he returned home in November of 1833 to much acclaim for his achievements there. He had opened up trade relations with Russia (although the treaty he negotiated turned out to be unsuccessful in the long term). He had met with so many powerful Europeans that he found his opinions to be in high demand in Washington. On the evening of his arrival back in Philadelphia, state leaders honored him with a formal dinner.

CHAPTER FOUR

SENATOR BUCHANAN

What, Sir! Prevent the American people from crossing the Rocky Mountains? You might as well command Niagara [Falls] not to flow. We must fulfill our destiny.

—Senator James Buchanan, in defense
of U.S. expansion westward

Back in Lancaster after his year in Russia, Buchanan had much to do. While in Saint Petersburg, he had left his law practice in the hands of two colleagues. These two lawyers not only took good care of Buchanan's office while he was away, but they also purchased a home for him—a former home of Robert Coleman, Ann's father. Once he had settled in, Buchanan threw himself back into his law practice. He maintained his interest in politics, and it was around this time that he began dreaming of one day being president.

Buchanan returned to the nation's capital in 1834 to serve in the Senate.

———————————— ◇ ————————————

In the autumn of 1834, the Pennsylvania legislature elected him to the U.S. Senate to fill a vacancy. So in December, Buchanan left his new home in the care of a housekeeper, Esther Parker, known as Miss Hetty. He returned to Washington, D.C., as Senator Buchanan, Democrat from Pennsylvania. Each state sends two senators to the Senate. Buchanan already knew many of his Senate colleagues from his time in the House of Representatives. By then the Federalist Party was entirely gone from the political scene. The majority party in the Senate was the Whig Party, which, like the Federalists, supported a strong central government.

BANK OF THE UNITED STATES

One of the major issues of the day was the continuation of the Second Bank of the United States. The Second Bank was a national bank that had existed since 1816. (The First Bank had operated from 1791 to 1811.) The bank issued paper money, made loans, and held deposits from businesses and the government.

———————————— ✧ ————————————

The Second Bank of the United States was located in Philadelphia, Pennsylvania. The building still stands, serving as a portrait gallery.

The national bank had the power to stop state banks from making loans to people without collateral (property or something else of value that borrowers promise to give up if they cannot repay the loans). Many farmers, especially in western and southern states, tried to get loans from state banks, but the national bank wouldn't approve the loans because the farmers lacked collateral. As a result, many farmers disliked the national bank. Although the issue was not divided strictly along party lines, many Democrats also disliked the bank because it put so much power in the hands of the federal government instead of the hands of individual states.

In particular, President Jackson and his supporters opposed the bank. The bank's charter (operating papers) was set to expire in 1836, and Congress would have to vote to renew it. When Congress voted to recharter the bank in 1832—four years earlier than needed—Jackson used his presidential veto power (the power to keep a bill from passing) to overturn the charter.

The bank was located in Philadelphia, Pennsylvania. The city had become a financial center because the bank was there, and this business helped all of Pennsylvania. This fact put Buchanan in an uncomfortable situation. As a Jacksonian Democrat, he was against the bank and did not want to vote to renew its charter in 1836. But as a representative of Pennsylvania, he knew that people in his state favored the bank, regardless of political party. Whichever way he voted, he would lose supporters—either voters at home or Democrats in Washington. Since he had national political ambitions, the issue was quite difficult for him. In the end, he sided with the Jacksonian Democrats and voted against renewing the bank's charter. The Democrats were successful in this vote, and the national bank shut down.

FAVORITE UNCLE

Ever since the death of his father and then his mother, Buchanan had assumed the role of head of the family for his younger brothers and sisters. He had paid for several of his siblings to attend school. Then, after several of his siblings died, he had taken care of their orphaned children. One niece, Harriet Lane, had been orphaned at the age of eleven. Buchanan assumed the role of parent and sent her to boarding school in Virginia. On vacations, she lived with Miss Hetty in Lancaster and visited Buchanan in Washington.

In 1838 Buchanan's brother-in-law died, leaving his sister Harriet with little money and a five-year-old son, James Buchanan Henry. Buchanan by then had purchased another house, the old family home in Mercersburg, and he divided his time between Mercersburg, Lancaster, and Washington, D.C. He invited Harriet and her son to live at the Mercersburg home. Soon another niece, suffering from tuberculosis, moved into the household. Buchanan's family members did not ask outright for his help, but Buchanan felt that it was his responsibility as the oldest living family member to help them.

SLAVERY AND NEW STATES

Back in Washington, two other issues dominated U.S. politics. The first was the enslavement of black Americans. The second was expansion, or adding new states to the Union. These issues came to be tied together politically.

Slave ships carried hundreds of Africans in cramped quarters.

Since colonial times, Americans had imported Africans as slaves to work on their farms and in their homes and businesses. Many Americans—called abolitionists—had called for an end to slavery. In the late 1700s, northern states began passing laws that gradually freed existing slaves and outlawed the importation of new slaves. In the South, where family-owned plantations (large farms) formed the backbone of the economy, slaves continued to provide necessary cheap labor.

The U.S. policy of westward expansion kept the slavery issue in the forefront of politics. White Americans continued to move west across North America, and they wanted to create new states in western lands. The United States continued to admit new states to the Union, and with each new state, the slavery question came up. To keep the peace between northerners who opposed slavery and southerners who supported it, Congress tried to balance the numbers of free states and slave states.

BUCHANAN'S VIEWS

Buchanan had distinct views on both slavery and expansion. Personally, he felt that slavery was morally wrong. His home state of Pennsylvania had gradually abolished slavery, starting in 1780. But Buchanan also felt that slave owners' rights had to be protected. He further believed that the inhabitants of new territories (areas under U.S. control that had not yet become states) should decide whether their territories would be free or slaveholding—an idea called popular sovereignty. Buchanan's position on western expansion was very clear: he believed that the United States should eventually occupy all of North America. He stated this position over and over, beginning in the 1830s.

With his experience as a foreign minister, Buchanan was named chairman of the Senate Foreign Relations Committee, the group of senators who dealt with adding new states to the Union. (At the time, Great Britain, Mexico, and Native Americans still controlled much of the West, so acquiring western territory was considered foreign relations.)

Manifest Destiny

A wagon train makes its way westward toward California.

◇

Beginning in the 1830s, Senator Buchanan was one of the first U.S. politicians to believe that the United States would eventually stretch across North America to the Pacific Ocean. By the 1840s, the vast majority of Americans felt the same way. This idea came to be called manifest destiny. John L. O'Sullivan, a newspaper reporter, first used the phrase *manifest destiny* in an article on Texas statehood in 1845.

Manifest means "obvious," and *destiny* refers to future events that are bound to happen. Together, the words reflected Americans' feeling that it was their God-given right to control the entire North American continent. Backers of manifest destiny also believed that U.S. economic and political systems were superior to all others. To them, U.S. superiority was further justification for the United States gaining control of the entire continent.

In the 1800s, the U.S. government based many of its policies on the idea of manifest destiny. The idea fueled the U.S. takeover of Native American lands and the killing or relocating of thousands of Native Americans in the process. It fueled the dispute with Great Britain over Oregon Territory. It also influenced U.S. dealings with Mexico.

In the 1840s and 1850s, the United States expanded a great deal:

- Texas became a state in 1845.
- In 1846 Great Britain handed over the section of Oregon Territory south of Canada—present-day Idaho, Oregon, and Washington and parts of Montana and Wyoming—to the United States.
- In 1848 the Treaty of Guadalupe Hidalgo ended the Mexican War (1846–1848). Under this treaty, the United States gained present-day California, Nevada, and Utah and parts of New Mexico, Arizona, Colorado, and Wyoming.
- With the Gadsden Purchase of 1853, the United States bought the southern edges of Arizona and New Mexico from Mexico.

In these ways, the United States came to own all the territory of its present states except Alaska (purchased from Russia in 1867) and Hawaii (annexed in 1898).

In the 1840s, both the United States and Great Britain claimed Oregon Territory. This tract of land occupied much of present-day western Canada as well as present-day Idaho, Oregon, and Washington and parts of present-day Montana and Wyoming. Some Americans thought the United States should allow Britain to occupy the northern part of Oregon and avoid a potential war over the territory. But ever since his days in Europe, Buchanan had distrusted the British. He was convinced they intended to colonize the remaining unsettled lands in North America. In the Senate, Buchanan argued strongly for the United States' right to own all of Oregon Territory.

At the same time, Buchanan argued for allowing Texas to join the Union. After revolting against Mexico, Texas had become an independent republic in 1836. Over the next nine years, the Republic of Texas asked to be admitted to the United States several times, but the slavery issue kept stalling the question. Southern leaders wanted Texas to be admitted, but northerners objected because Texas allowed slavery.

In 1844 the Senate considered a treaty that would make Texas a state. Buchanan warned his fellow senators that if they voted against Texas statehood, the Republic of Texas would turn to Great Britain and become an enemy of the United States. In a private Senate hearing, Buchanan asked his colleagues, "Shall Texas become part of our glorious confederacy? Shall she be bone of our bone and flesh of our flesh; or shall she become a dangerous and hostile rival?"

Buchanan's primary interest was in expanding the United States, and his answer to the slavery question in Texas was intended to make both sides happy. He suggested dividing

Texas into five states: two slaveholding and three free. This proposal displeased the northern states, which did not want to allow any new slave states. The treaty did not pass the Senate, but Buchanan's reputation as an expansionist was firmly made. Also made was his reputation for favoring the South in the slavery debate.

Buchanan served as secretary of state from 1845 through 1848.

CHAPTER FIVE

DIPLOMACY

My life is that of a galley [shipboard] slave.
I have not read thirty consecutive pages
in any book since I came into the
Department of State.
—Secretary of State James Buchanan

By 1844 James Buchanan had established himself as a powerful voice in the U.S. Senate, with ten years' experience. He was also heavily involved in presidential politics. Many Democrats wanted to make expansion the key issue in the next presidential election. As a strong advocate of this policy, Buchanan seemed like an ideal candidate for president in 1844. Supporters in the Democratic Party suggested that he run.

Buchanan, however, sensed that he would not have enough support to win the election, so he withdrew his name from consideration. He was very interested in being president, but he wanted to wait until the right time—until he felt he could win an election. The Democratic Party ended up nominating James K. Polk, a former congressman and Tennessee governor. Buchanan campaigned hard for Polk during the election year.

In November 1844, Polk was elected president. As a reward for his support, Polk named Buchanan his secretary of state—a position often considered to be the second most important one in the U.S. government, after the job of president. In 1845 Buchanan resigned from the Senate and began the secretary of state job for President Polk.

James K. Polk

———— ◇ ————

BORDER DISPUTES

As secretary of state, Buchanan was responsible for the country's relations with the rest of the world. He was in charge of negotiating treaties with other countries and settling disputes between the United States and other nations. Since the United States was acquiring much new territory and admitting many new states during this period, Buchanan was kept busy in his new post.

One of his first tasks concerned Oregon Territory. The boundary dispute with Great Britain remained. As a senator, Buchanan had argued that the United States was entitled to the entire territory—whether or not this position would launch a war with Britain. But as secretary of state, Buchanan was more sensitive to the dangers of war, and he agreed to a compromise with the British. In an agreement made in 1846, Britain took control of Oregon Territory north of the 49th parallel (the present-day U.S.-Canadian border) and the United States took the territory to the south.

Another issue from Buchanan's days in the Senate—Texas— was also waiting for him when he became secretary of state. In 1845, after much debate, Congress had finally voted to admit Texas to the Union as a slave state. But Mexico still claimed Texas as its own and had threatened to break off friendly relations with the United States if Texas were admitted. What's more, the two nations could not agree on the Texas-Mexico border. In 1846 the dispute turned into the Mexican War.

——————————— ✧ ———————————

In September 1846, U.S. troops advance in the Battle of Monterrey in the Mexican War.

While U.S. and Mexican armies clashed, Buchanan spent much of the next two years negotiating with Mexico over boundaries.

On the battlefield, the U.S. forces proved superior, and in 1848 Mexico surrendered. Buchanan helped draft the peace treaty, the Treaty of Guadalupe Hidalgo, at war's end. Under this agreement, Mexico gave up all claims to Texas and also handed over to the United States present-day California, Nevada, and Utah, and parts of New Mexico, Arizona, Colorado, and Wyoming. The United States was growing quickly.

Buchanan was also kept busy by events in Europe. Civil unrest occurred in both France and Germany in 1848, and as secretary of state, Buchanan recognized new governments in those countries. At the request of President Polk, Buchanan attempted to buy Cuba, an island near the southern coast of Florida, from Spain. But negotiations with Spain failed.

——————— ✧ ———————

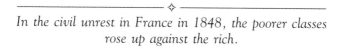

In the civil unrest in France in 1848, the poorer classes rose up against the rich.

WHEATLAND

Another presidential election took place in 1848, and Buchanan hoped to become the Democratic nominee. But in May, at the party's national convention, representatives instead selected Senator Lewis Cass of Michigan. Buchanan was disappointed, but he immediately began preparing to win the 1852 nomination.

Meanwhile, he was becoming more and more unhappy with his job as secretary of state. He wrote to a friend that he was overworked. He also felt that for all the hard work required of him, he was not advancing in his political career as much as wanted. At the same time, he developed several health problems, including a nervous tic in his leg and a painful tumor in his nose that required many operations.

Buchanan wanted to move out of Lancaster. For one thing, he needed a larger home to accommodate visits from his twenty-two nieces and nephews. And since he was thinking about running for president, he also wanted a more private residence. He knew it would be hard to live in the middle of Lancaster while leading a presidential campaign. His Lancaster home was just down the street from the newspaper office. He worried that reporters and the public would constantly be bothering him.

So in 1848, Buchanan purchased a country estate near Lancaster. This grand mansion had been built in 1828 for William Jenkins, a wealthy Lancaster lawyer and banker. Jenkins had named the estate the Wheatlands because of the lush wheat fields that surrounded the property. Buchanan bought the mansion, several guesthouses, and twenty-two acres of land for $6,750. He shortened the name of the estate to Wheatland. He loved the estate and

Wheatland was a grand estate.

———————————— ✧ ————————————

called it the "ideal of a statesman's abode." He appreciated "the comforts and tranquility of home as contrasted with the troubles, perplexities, and difficulties [of public life]."

The same autumn that Buchanan bought Wheatland, Zachary Taylor of the Whig Party was elected president of the United States. Taylor soon appointed a new secretary of state, and Buchanan, by then fifty-eight years old, left Washington and moved to Wheatland full-time.

His favorite niece Harriet, by then eighteen years old, had finished boarding school and had became part of his household. She lived at Wheatland with Miss Hetty and a few other nieces and nephews. Harriet was given the task of decorating the mansion and acting as its hostess. Together,

James and Harriet threw lavish parties and balls, entertaining many important people who lived in or visited Pennsylvania. Buchanan became well known for his grand parties and social events. Although considered an eligible bachelor, he was content with the companionship of his family and close friends and did not pursue any women romantically.

For the next year, Buchanan lived at Wheatland and practiced law in Lancaster. However, he did not give up his presidential ambitions, and he kept up with political events. In 1850 Congress passed a series of acts aimed at settling the slavery issue. Known as the Compromise of 1850, the acts allowed California to enter the Union as a free state. The acts also created the territories of New Mexico and Utah but left the slavery question for the settlers in those territories to vote upon. Finally, the compromise included the Fugitive Slave Law, which helped slave owners retrieve runaway slaves. The Fugitive Slave Law pleased the South but angered many in the North.

President Taylor died in July 1850, and his vice president, Millard Fillmore, took over as president. That same year, Buchanan began his pursuit of the next Democratic presidential nomination with a letter to party leaders. In the letter, he discussed his political views. He said he had doubts about leaving the slavery decision to ordinary and sometimes uneducated citizens, but he still believed that letting settlers vote was the best way to avoid bloodshed over the slavery question. He also expressed his support for the new Fugitive Slave Law. This position was geared specifically to picking up southern backing for his presidential bid, and it worked. Buchanan was becoming known as proslavery.

Ultimately, he was disappointed in his bid for the presidential nomination. In 1852 the Democrats nominated Franklin Pierce—a former army general with support in both northern and southern states. Buchanan began preparing for the next presidential race.

TO LONDON

In early 1853, Franklin Pierce was sworn in as the fourteenth U.S. president. Buchanan remained at Wheatland and became president of the board of trustees of Franklin and Marshall College in Lancaster. He soon received word from President Pierce, asking him to become minister to Great Britain.

✧ —————————————

Buchanan served as the minister to Great Britain under President Franklin Pierce (left).

Buchanan certainly had the background in foreign affairs for this post. But he was afraid that by accepting it and living in Britain for four years, he would lose his chance at being nominated for president in 1856. After much consideration, however, he accepted the job, knowing that to turn it down might damage his political career. The Senate confirmed his appointment the next day. Buchanan's hometown newspaper, the *Lancaster Intelligencer*, praised the new British minister as "a gentleman of exalted worth, a scholar of rare attainments, and a statesman of enlarged views and great experience."[17]

Buchanan arrived in London on August 13, 1853. Soon after, he was formally presented to Queen Victoria, Britain's ruler. "She has not many personal charms, but is gracious and dignified in her manners and her character is without blemish," he wrote home to his niece Harriet. Harriet was eager to hear all about London and planned to come live with her uncle once he found a suitable home to rent.

Meanwhile, Buchanan caused a stir in British society when he refused to appear in the official gold-laced suit required in front of the queen. Most U.S. diplomats dressed in this formal outfit for court visits. But, following orders issued by the secretary of state in Washington, Buchanan instead met the queen wearing a plain black suit. By dressing up his outfit with a black-handled sword, Buchanan was able to escape the queen's displeasure. Nevertheless, the London newspaper the *Herald* made fun of him as "the gentleman in the black coat from Yankeeland."

When news of Buchanan's stand on this issue reached the United States, the *Harrisburg Patriot* praised him for refusing "to decorate himself with . . . trappings and tinsel." In the end, his refusal to wear formal dress bolstered his

By the time of Buchanan's appointment, Victoria (right) had already been queen for sixteen years.
——————— ◇

popularity among voters at home. As a friend wrote to him, "Although a small matter, nothing you have ever done has given you so great a hold on the masses of the people of all parties." To Buchanan, who more than anything wanted to be elected president in 1856, this was welcome news.

Minister Buchanan had issues besides dress facing him during his time in London. One of the most important was a dispute between the United States and Great Britain over a planned canal across Central America to link the Atlantic and Pacific oceans. In 1850 the two countries had signed the Clayton-Bulwer Treaty, which said that both nations would share in the protection of land around the proposed canal that was to run through Nicaragua. But a dispute soon arose as to how much territory was included in the agreement. As minister to Great Britain, Buchanan tried to get Britain to give up the territory in question, but he failed. While Buchanan's job in London was to deal with U.S.-British relations, the task he may be best remembered for in that period had seemingly little to do with Great Britain. It involved the future of the island of Cuba. This island, located about ninety miles off the Florida coast, had been owned by Spain since the 1500s. But Cuba's citizens were unhappy with Spanish rule and wanted to wage a revolution. If that happened, the United States thought that Great Britain—a longtime ally of Spain—might gain control of the island.

This situation concerned the United States for one main reason: slaves. Cuba was a slaveholding territory, and Great Britain was strongly antislavery. The United States worried that either the slaves in Cuba would rise up against their owners or the British government would free them. Then, U.S. leaders feared, slaves in the United States might hear about the freeing of the slaves in Cuba and begin to revolt against their owners.

When he was secretary of state, Buchanan had tried to get Spain to sell Cuba to the United States. President Pierce asked Buchanan, along with the U.S. ministers to France and Spain, to pursue the idea again. The three ministers met in October 1854 in Ostend, Belgium, to discuss the situation. They took a break and met again in France. There, they drafted a report to President Pierce, telling him that the United States should offer to buy

Cuba. The report also warned that, if Spain refused to sell, U.S. forces might have to seize the island by force to prevent the freeing of Cuba's slaves.

Then the press got hold of the report (called the Ostend Manifesto), which was meant to be private. Newspapers wrote that Buchanan and his colleagues recommended taking Cuba by force. The idea caused outrage, especially among northerners who feared the government was trying to expand slavery militarily. The resulting bad publicity for Buchanan was unfair, since he had not actually recommended seizing the island. The situation embarrassed Buchanan, but it did come with a silver lining for him. Since the aim of acquiring Cuba in the first place was to help southern slave owners, Buchanan did gain some additional political support from proslavery southerners.

THE KANSAS-NEBRASKA ACT

While Buchanan was in London, the slavery debate in the United States raged on. For years, people had been settling in the territories of Kansas and Nebraska. People in both territories wanted statehood. But they were held up by one big question: should the new states allow slaves or not? Northerners wanted the states to be free. But one Missouri senator said he would "sink in hell" before he allowed Kansas to enter the Union as a free state.

Senator Stephen A. Douglas of Illinois thought he had the solution to the Kansas-Nebraska question. He offered a bill that would allow residents there to decide the question for themselves once the territories became states— that is, he called for popular sovereignty. This idea pleased

many people in the South, because it meant Kansas and
Nebraska might become slave states. But abolitionists
opposed the bill, which directly violated the Missouri
Compromise, an 1820 law that had prohibited slavery
north of a certain boundary.

In 1854, after a long and bitter debate in Congress,
Douglas's Kansas-Nebraska Act passed, but northerners were
outraged. A mob in Illinois nearly killed Senator Douglas.
Most northern Democratic congressmen who had supported
the bill were voted out in the next election.

─────────── ✧

*Stephen Douglas,
author of the Kansas-
Nebraska Act*

Serving in London, Buchanan avoided the turmoil of the Kansas-Nebraska Act and never publicly took sides in the debate. But embarrassed by both the Ostend Manifesto and his failure in negotiations over Central America, Buchanan asked President Pierce if he could end his appointment early. With the president's permission, he set sail for the United States in April 1856.

CHAPTER SIX

THE MOST SUITABLE MAN
FOR THE TIMES

*Never did a wily politician so industriously
plot and plan to secure a nomination than
Mr. Buchanan did in his. . . hunt
for the Presidency.*

—Journalist Benjamin Perley Poore

During the two-week voyage back to the United States, Buchanan reflected on the possibility of finally receiving the Democratic nomination for president. The election was coming up in the fall of 1856. He had heard from several friends that he was in a good position to earn the nomination that year. After all his years of hoping for the presidency, he began to think that when at last it seemed he might be successful, he was not so certain he wanted it.

After years of increasing tensions between North and South, the United States was on the brink of civil war. The president's job over the next four years would not be an easy one. Buchanan must have been thinking of the potential for a quiet retirement at Wheatland versus the strains of leading a country on the verge of war when he wrote to his niece Harriet. He quoted a French saying: "The things we want the most do not seem to happen, or, when they do, they are neither at the right time or in the right manner to make us happy."

Buchanan decided to neither encourage nor discourage his supporters from advancing his name as the Democratic nominee. He may have begun to rethink this desire in light of the troubled state of the Union. Or perhaps, as some historians say, he was simply too proud to campaign outright for the nomination, after being disappointed so many times in the past.

Buchanan disembarked from the steamship *Arago* in New York City, one day after his sixty-fifth birthday. He discouraged his supporters from throwing him a large

✧ ————————————
The Arago *carried*
Buchanan *home from*
London *in 1856.*

public welcome dinner. At such a dinner, he knew, he would have to give a speech—and that would undoubtedly be interpreted as campaigning. Instead, the returning minister had a quiet dinner with friends, including the city's mayor. A few days later, he headed by train for Philadelphia, where he was greeted with a booming cannon, a parade, and fireworks. A private train draped with signs saying "Welcome home, Pennsylvania's favorite son!" took him home to Lancaster the next morning.

Despite his apparent lack of enthusiasm for the presidential nomination, Buchanan soon found himself to be his party's favorite candidate. His popularity sprung not so much from his record of public service as from his lack of direct involvement in the slavery debate while he was in Britain. During those years, the rift between North and South and between slavery supporters and abolitionists, had gotten larger. Some southern states even talked of seceding (withdrawing) from the Union if slavery were outlawed. Most of the country's leading politicians had been forced to take a stand on one side or the other, thereby losing support from the other side. By being in Britain, Buchanan had largely remained out of the argument.

THE RUN FOR PRESIDENT

By 1856 there was no sign that the tensions caused by the Kansas-Nebraska Act were fading. In fact, as settlers poured into the new territories, the situation grew much worse. In Kansas southerners set up a proslavery government in the town of Lecompton, and a group known as the Free Staters set up an antislavery government in Topeka. Soon fighting broke out. Within a few months, more than two hundred

*Five people died in this incident of proslavery citizens attacking
Free Staters. It was one of many fights in the Kansas civil
war that gave the territory the name Bleeding Kansas.*

---

people were killed in this statewide civil war. The territory
became known as Bleeding Kansas.

Just weeks after the outbreak of fighting in Kansas, the
Democratic Party met in Cincinnati to nominate its candidate for president. Some northern Democrats wanted
President Pierce as their candidate again, but his reputation
had been damaged by the Ostend Manifesto. Some southern members wanted Senator Douglas, who had proposed
the Kansas-Nebraska Act.

But with Bleeding Kansas at the forefront of national
attention, James Buchanan was the obvious choice. He
was satisfactory to southerners because he had supported
popular sovereignty in the past. He was also satisfactory
to the North because he had never publicly supported the

Kansas-Nebraska Act (since he had been in Great Britain during its passage). Buchanan won the nomination. The party chose John C. Breckinridge of Kentucky as its candidate for vice president.

At home in Wheatland, Buchanan received word of his nomination in a telegram. He wrote back to party leaders that he was honored and humbled to be chosen. He also wrote of his intentions if elected: to help heal the Union and to preserve peace and friendship with all nations. Interestingly, his acceptance letter stressed his hopes for improving foreign relations above his hopes for uniting the country. After all, he had been nominated largely because of his absence from the United States during the fight over slavery, not because of any proposed policies for dealing with the tensions.

This campaign poster from 1856 shows Buchanan and his running mate, John C. Breckinridge.

Once Buchanan received the nomination, most Democrats rallied around him. Worried that some southern states would follow through on their threats to secede from the Union, the party tried to appeal to voters who wanted to save the Union above all else. It tried to stay away from the issue of slavery and talked instead about keeping the country whole. Throughout the election, Buchanan gave no public speeches, but from Wheatland he wrote hundreds of letters to newspapers and supporters, stressing the importance of keeping the Union together. "The union is in danger and the people everywhere begin to know it," he wrote.

Buchanan's strongest opponent was a former senator from California, John C. Frémont, the Republican candidate. The Republican Party was a new party of people opposed to slavery. Many former Democrats and Whigs—still the country's two largest political parties—had joined the Republicans. During the 1856 campaign, the Republicans spoke about the evils of slavery and the necessity of keeping slavery out of any new territories.

✧ ————————

This presidential campaign banner promotes John C. Frémont, famous for his exploring expeditions in the Rocky Mountains.

Frémont was very popular in the North, where cities were filled with Republican campaign posters with sayings like: "Free Speech, Free Press, Free Soil, Free Men, Frémont and Victory!" Meanwhile, Buchanan and other Democrats portrayed Republicans as wanting to break up the Union. "The Republicans must be, as they can be with justice, boldly assailed as disunionists, and this charge must be reiterated again and again," Buchanan wrote. Buchanan's other opponent was former president Millard Fillmore, supported by both the Whig and the American parties. (The American Party, nicknamed the Know-Nothing Party, opposed immigration and Catholicism, the religion of many immigrants.)

Although the three major candidates ran as nominees of specific political parties, parties meant little in the election of 1856. The election came down to proslavery versus antislavery and saving the Union versus separating the country on the slavery issue.

In the end, Buchanan won the election. He did not receive a majority of votes from the people. He received about 1.8 million votes, Frémont about 1.3 million, and Fillmore about 900,000, but he won a large majority in the Electoral College vote.

VICTORY

At Wheatland, Buchanan received the news of his victory. As he celebrated with his niece and a few friends, many people around the country also rejoiced. Although several southern states had been threatening to leave the Union, Americans felt they would not do so with Buchanan in the White House. Buchanan still had a strong reputation for being pro-South. As one of his friends wrote shortly after the election, "I believe now that no other man but Mr. Buchanan could have been elected. He was The Man . . . the most suitable man for the times."

Immediately after the election, Wheatland became a tourist attraction. People from all over the country came to Lancaster to see where the new president lived. One newspaper reported that Buchanan was receiving four hundred visitors a day. (Most historians agree that the figure was an exaggeration.)

Buchanan would not take office for several months, but he had plenty of work to do until then. First on his agenda was picking his cabinet—his closest advisers, such as the secretary of state and secretary of the treasury. All presidents appoint their supporters and people with similar political views to cabinet posts. Picking a cabinet is often a time to reward party members who were loyal during the campaign.

——————————— ✦ ———————————

Buchanan (center, with his hand on the book) *and his cabinet*

But Buchanan was extremely careful in picking his cabinet, and he kept one theme in mind: only strong supporters of the Union would receive posts. He also attempted to balance his appointments between northerners and southerners, but to most observers, he demonstrated a preference for the South. Although he had won the presidency on his appeal to keep the country united, his reputation as a southern supporter was growing stronger.

DRED SCOTT

Slavery was on everyone's mind during the winter of 1856–1857. But Buchanan was determined to wait until he was sworn in as president before taking a strong stand on the issue. He knew that the question that threatened to break up the Union had no easy answer. But in February, he found reason to hope that there might be an easy answer after all because the Supreme Court was about to decide the Dred Scott case.

Dred Scott

Dred Scott was an African American man and a slave. In 1846 he had sued for his freedom and for his wife's freedom on the grounds that they had lived for a time in a free state and a free territory. In 1850 a court in Saint Louis, Missouri, declared the Scotts to be free. But two years later, the Missouri Supreme Court (the state's highest court) reversed that decision, and the Scotts were slaves once again. By 1857 the Dred Scott case was on the docket of the U.S. Supreme Court—the highest court in the nation.

The court had two difficult questions to examine. First, was Scott a slave or a free man? And, if he were a slave, did he even have the right to sue in federal court? Furthermore, the court would look at Congress's power to prohibit slavery in U.S. territories.

As Inauguration Day grew nearer, Buchanan hoped that the Supreme Court would decide the Dred Scott case before he became president. In this way, the court, not Buchanan and Congress, would make the tough decisions about slavery. At Wheatland, Buchanan waited for word from the court and tried to work out the details of his final cabinet appointments.

CHAPTER SEVEN

PRESIDENT BUCHANAN

What is right and what is [feasible]
are two different things."
—James Buchanan

Most of Lancaster was awake long before 6:00 A.M. on March 2, 1857. The morning was bitter cold and snowy, but hundreds of people filled the streets. At six the church bells began ringing. It was time for President-elect Buchanan to begin his journey from Wheatland to the Lancaster train station and on to the nation's capital. A band led a parade from the town to Buchanan's estate. But after about five minutes in the freezing cold, the band members had to abandon their instruments and climb into a wagon. At Wheatland the parade waited for Buchanan, his niece Harriet, his nephew James Buchanan Henry, and Miss Hetty to board their carriage. Then the procession made its way to the station, where a special train had been decorated with scenes from Wheatland and red, white, and blue symbols.

Buchanan's train stopped first in Baltimore, where a banquet lunch took place at Barnum's Hotel. Unfortunately, the president-elect was sick with a stomach virus. He spent most of the time upstairs, resting in one of the hotel's suites. In mid-afternoon, he boarded another train for Washington. There, he stayed at the National Hotel for two nights. On March 4, he would take up residence at the White House.

INAUGURATION FESTIVITIES

Buchanan awoke on March 4, Inauguration Day, still ill with a stomach virus. He swallowed medicine prescribed by his doctor and began to dress. He would wear a plain black suit to show that he understood the seriousness of the situation. The country was on the brink of disunion over the slavery issue. Buchanan wanted the people to see him as grave and dignified and able to keep the Union together. For Buchanan personally, the day marked the culmination of a longtime dream: becoming president of the United States. The lining of his suit coat reflected his joy, with a brilliant pattern of thirty-one stars representing the states of the Union at that time.

For many years, tensions had been mounting, and on this day, Americans were eager for something to celebrate. Thousands of people poured into the nation's capital for the inauguration. Every hotel was full. People slept in hallways, on couches, and any other place they could find. The morning was sunny and clear, and a feeling of excitement filled the city.

Buchanan stood in front of the eastern entrance to the Capitol to be sworn in as the fifteenth president of the United States. In his speech, he declared he was "convinced that I owe my election to the inherent love for the Constitution and the Union which still animates the hearts of the American people." He clarified his support for popular sovereignty as the way to decide the slavery question in the territories, and he spoke of his hope that "the long agitation on this subject . . . will speedily become extinct." When Buchanan finished speaking, the chief justice of the Supreme Court performed the swearing-in ceremony, and the event was over.

That evening hundreds of people crowded into a temporary building on Judiciary Square for the inaugural ball. The white ballroom ceiling was covered with gold stars representing the Union, and the walls were decorated in red, white, and blue. One partygoer later wrote, "Such a jam, such heat . . . I never either saw or felt before."

———————————— ✧ ————————————

Buchanan and his niece Harriet greeted guests at the inaugural ball.

*Buchanan was sixty-five years old when he began
his presidency in March 1857.*

Buchanan and his niece Harriet Lane mingled with the
crowd, then made their way to their new house at 1600
Pennsylvania Avenue—the White House. Buchanan's
nephew James Buchanan Henry would live with them
there too.

AT HOME IN THE WHITE HOUSE

For years it seemed that the nation's capital had been
gloomy. Not only was the country mired in the divisive
slavery issue, but the White House itself had had a
somber tone for more than ten years. President John
Tyler's wife and President Pierce's son had died during

their terms in office. President Polk's wife was a strict Presbyterian who had banned all dancing and liquor from the White House. And President Taylor's wife had refused to socialize with politicians, who she felt were beneath her socially. As a result, it had been many years since grand balls or parties had taken place in the White House.

But with the arrival of the Buchanans, people sensed that Washington social life was about to get much more exciting. The new president—sometimes called by the nickname Old Buck—enjoyed fine food and drink. He once complained to a liquor merchant that the White House needed more champagne: "Pints are very inconvenient in this house, as [champagne] is not used in such small quantities." Once, when Britain's Prince of Wales visited the White House, he brought such a large group with him that Buchanan had to sleep in a hallway to make room for his guests. Harriet Lane enjoyed hosting lavish parties and became a central figure in Washington society.

─────────── ✧

Harriet Lane served as hostess of the White House during Buchanan's presidency.

Harriet Lane, First Niece

Harriet Lane was the daughter of James Buchanan's sister Jane and her husband, Elliot Tole Lane. Harriet, known as Hal for most of her life, was born in 1830 and orphaned in 1841 at the age of eleven.

Upon the death of her parents, Hal was informally adopted by Buchanan, who sent her first to boarding schools in Lancaster, Pennsylvania, and Charleston, West Virginia, and then to the Georgetown Visitation Convent, a women's college near Washington, D.C. She graduated from the convent with honors and soon moved with her uncle to his newly acquired Wheatland estate. Buchanan treated Hal as his own daughter and gave her the responsibility of running his household. She picked out most of the furnishings for Wheatland and became a successful entertainer, planning many formal dinners and dances at the estate.

When Buchanan was appointed ambassador to Great Britain in 1853, Hal joined him. At the age of twenty-three, she was considered a great beauty, with long golden curls and a talent for witty and flirtatious conversation. She impressed Queen Victoria and became a frequent guest at royal events.

When Buchanan became president, Hal served as his First Lady. In this position, she promoted many social causes, including hospital and prison reform. She was also one of the first people in Washington to speak out about the plight of Native Americans. She felt it was unfair for the United States to take over Native American land, noting that Indians had lived on the land for centuries. She argued for the government to repay Native Americans for their land in some way. She also supported the arts and organized evening concerts at the White House.

From her teenage years, Hal was popular and flirted happily with many suitors. Buchanan often warned her against rushing into marriage, and she waited until she was almost thirty-six to marry. With her uncle's approval, she chose Henry Johnston, a lawyer from a wealthy Baltimore family. Hal and Henry were married in the parlor at Wheatland on January 11, 1866. After her marriage, Hal moved to Baltimore, where her first son, James Buchanan Johnston, was born.

After Buchanan's death, Hal inherited Wheatland, which she maintained as a summer residence. In 1870 her second son, Henry Johnston II, was born. In 1881 the eldest son died of rheumatic fever at the age of fourteen. In 1882 thirteen-year-old Henry died of the same illness. Following the death of their two sons, the Johnstons founded the Harriet Lane Home for Invalid Children in Baltimore. This home for children with chronic diseases was the first such institute for sick children in the United States. It later became a teaching and research center at the Johns Hopkins School of Medicine.

In 1884 Hal's husband Henry died suddenly of pneumonia. Following the loss of her family, Harriet sold both Wheatland and her Baltimore home and moved to a townhouse in Washington, D.C. She spent the rest of her life involved in charitable causes. On July 3, 1903, Harriet died of cancer at a summer resort in Rhode Island.

Once every week, Buchanan hosted a state dinner for about forty guests, working his way through a guest list that included Supreme Court justices, ambassadors, senators, representatives, and other important dignitaries. Harriet managed all the details, including ordering the menu from the White House chef and making the seating arrangements to ensure that political enemies were kept apart. Most important, she tried to balance the guest lists between northerners and southerners. (Still, many critics complained that Buchanan entertained more southerners than northerners in the White House.) About once a month, Harriet planned elaborate formal balls for one hundred or more guests, including any foreign leaders

Buchanan had great interest in foreign affairs. Here he welcomes ambassadors from Japan at a formal reception.

who were visiting Washington. Buchanan added a greenhouse to the White House to grow flowers for these affairs. It seemed that celebration had returned to the nation's capital.

But life at the White House consisted of more than social events, and the new president quickly developed a daily routine. Every morning he woke at 6:30 and had breakfast with his niece and nephew. By 8:00 A.M., he was working in his second-floor office. He stayed there until noon. After lunch he met with his cabinet to discuss the day's most pressing issues. Then he took an hour's walk around Washington, usually strolling through Lafayette Square and the residential area north of the White House. Dinner was almost always at 7:00 P.M. Afterward, he would retire to his study. There he would read his daily mail, sorted into folders by his nephew James. Buchanan would go through the folders, answering the most important letters and sending the rest back to James to answer the next day. Finally, the president would often spend an hour before bedtime reading the Bible. He was not usually in bed before midnight.

In his years as president, Buchanan drew on lessons he had learned long before at his father's general store. He was well known for his orderly records and his attention to detail, especially details involving numbers and money. Once during his presidency, he discovered that he had underpaid a bill for expensive food by three cents. Although the three cents probably meant nothing to the food supplier, Buchanan insisted on sending him the money. He explained that he wished to pay neither too much nor too little but exactly what he owed.

TROUBLE SIMMERS

President Buchanan quickly settled in at the White House, but across the country, large issues remained unsettled. Tensions over slavery were increasing to the boiling point. Two days after Buchanan's inauguration, the Supreme Court ruled that as a black man Dred Scott was not a U.S. citizen and therefore could not sue for his freedom in federal court. This ruling angered abolitionists across the country. Their anger was also aimed at the new president, who supported the court's decision.

Meanwhile, troubles in Kansas continued. The proslavery movement, with its government in the town of Lecompton, continued to fight with antislavery settlers, with their own government in Topeka. Soon after Buchanan took office, Lecompton's government drafted a state constitution. If the constitution were approved by the territory's voters and then by Congress, Kansas could join the Union as a state. Under the Lecompton constitution, the new state would permit slavery.

But when the constitution came before voters, antislavery settlers refused to vote on the document because they did not recognize the government in Lecompton. With only proslavery settlers voting, the Lecompton group easily won approval of their constitution, which they then sent to Congress. President Buchanan, hoping to avoid more turmoil, recommended that Congress accept the Lecompton constitution and admit Kansas. This position angered northern congressmen and the antislavery public.

In the end, Congress did not approve the constitution but sent it back to the voters in Kansas, who defeated it at the polls in 1858. But the damage to Buchanan's reputation was done. Northerners felt they could not trust this new president.

In the U.S. congressional elections of 1858, voters elected enough antislavery candidates to take the majority in both the House and the Senate. The new congressmen were hostile to the president because of his stand on the Kansas question. And since the president needed congressional approval for almost any law he wished to pass, this hostility made it hard for Buchanan to get much accomplished.

And the new president had plenty he wanted to accomplish. He had campaigned on his promise to hold the Union together, but in fact, he was not seriously interested in issues such as slavery. He felt much more passionate about relations with other countries, specifically the idea of manifest destiny. According to this belief, the United States would be a great superpower, whose boundaries would stretching from the Atlantic Ocean to the Pacific Ocean and which no nation in the rest of the world could challenge.

He spent much of his time working on policies that would contribute to this goal. But with a hostile Congress, many of his ideas were voted down. Congress refused to approve his plans for a larger army and navy, to build a railroad across the continent, and to begin work on a canal and roads across Central America. For his part, Buchanan used his veto power to block several bills that Congress approved, including one that would have given free land to settlers in western territories.

Union soldiers march into battle.

CHAPTER EIGHT

MARCH TOWARD WAR

[There is] an incurable disease in the
public mind which may . . . terminate, at
last, in an open war by the North
to abolish slavery in the South.

—President Buchanan, in his 1859 State of the
Union message to the Senate

As President Buchanan's term in office progressed, tempers around the country were rising. Many people believed that a civil war was inevitable. Fighting was ongoing in Kansas. Even in the Senate chamber, violence became common enough that members began carrying pistols and knives for their own safety. In fact, one southern congressman had beaten a northern senator with his cane after the senator had made insulting remarks about the congressman's proslavery uncle, also a senator.

Buchanan tried to remain apart from the bitter quarrels over slavery, but he could not avoid the issue. People on both sides of the debate studied his every action. Did the president invite more southerners than northerners to visit the White House? He did! He must be proslavery, thought many northerners. Southerners leveled similar charges.

TROUBLE IN CENTRAL AMERICA

Instead of dealing with slavery, Buchanan continued to focus on foreign affairs, where his real talents lay. He worked tirelessly to improve relations with Great Britain, and he saw success when Britain signed treaties with several Central American countries that were beneficial to the United States. For example, these treaties finally settled the dispute with Britain that Buchanan had tried to end during his time as minister there in the 1850s.

But more problems continued in Central America. Many of the regions leaders ruled by fear. In some Central American nations, it was not uncommon to hear gunshots in city streets. In fact, the region was so disorderly that many European nations threatened to send troops to protect the safety of their citizens living there. But Buchanan felt it was important to keep European armies out of the Americas. He wanted to ensure U.S. dominance in the Western Hemisphere. Instead, he wanted the United States to send its own troops to Central America to act as a police force. But Congress, still hostile to Buchanan's proslavery reputation, refused to follow his suggestion.

Congress did not defeat all Buchanan's foreign affairs plans, however. During his four years as president, he had many successes. He convinced Great Britain to stop searching U.S. ships at sea. He also convinced France to give up its claim to French-born people who became U.S.

By Telegraph from England.

THE QUEEN'S MESSAGE,
THE PRESIDENT'S REPLY.

LONDON, ENG., August 12, 1858.

To HON. JAMES BUCHANAN, P. U. S.

Come, let us talk together. American genius and English enterprise have this day joined together, the *old* and the *new* world. Let us hope that they may be as closely allied in the bonds of peace, harmony, and kindred feeling.

VICTORIA.

BEDFORD SPRINGS, AUG. 12, 1858.

To Victoria,

Queen of England.

New England accepts with gladness, the hand of fellowship proffered by old England, and if ever discord or diversity of interest should threaten this alliance, let our language be, "entreat me not to leave thee, or return from following thee," for the interests of thy people shall be the interests of my people, and "thy God shall be my God."

JAMES BUCHANAN.

Buchanan's positive relationship with Queen Victoria helped him succeed in his negotiations with Great Britain.

citizens. All in all, President Buchanan increased the reputation of the United States in foreign circles at least as much as any other president before him had.

BITTER ELECTION

By 1860 the country was bitterly divided over slavery. Buchanan's term was coming to an end, and it was time for the major political parties to nominate candidates for the next election. Buchanan knew that the next president would likely have to oversee a civil war, and he did not want that job. In any event, his prosouthern reputation eliminated the possibility of his party renominating him. The Democrats needed a candidate who could appeal to both northerners and southerners.

But the Democratic Party was just as divided as the rest of the country. At the party's convention that year in Charleston, South Carolina, representatives from eight southern states walked out because the majority refused to endorse slavery. Those eight states nominated their own candidate, Vice President John Breckinridge. The northern representatives nominated Senator Stephen Douglas of Illinois.

At the same time, a new party, the Constitutional Union Party, nominated Senator John Bell of Tennessee. The Republicans meanwhile nominated former congressman Abraham Lincoln of Illinois. To confuse things even more, the Republican candidate for vice president was a former Democrat, Senator Hannibal Hamlin.

✧ ————————————

*Abraham Lincoln (left)
agreed with Buchanan
that the Union must be
kept together.*

The campaign of 1860 was focused entirely on slavery. Breckinridge was proslavery. Douglas believed in popular sovereignty. Lincoln was not antislavery, but he was dedicated to saving the Union and insisted that slavery could not spread to new states. Lincoln thought that if slavery were prevented from spreading, it would eventually die out. But if it were allowed into new states, it would destroy the Union.

Proslavery Democrats suspected that Lincoln was more antislavery than he claimed to be. They warned that if Lincoln were elected, he would free the slaves and the country would fall apart. Specifically, Democrats tried to frighten working-class white people with the idea that freed African Americans would take their jobs. In the end, it was the divided Democratic Party that put Lincoln in office. Taken together, Lincoln's three opponents received more than one million votes more than he did. But since those votes were divided among the three of them, Lincoln easily won the election.

SECESSION

With Lincoln's election, many in the South felt that their way of life—dependent on slave labor—would soon come to an end. This fear was perhaps greatest in South Carolina. The state (and others) had warned that it would leave the Union if Lincoln were elected. On December 20, 1860, just a month and a half after the election, South Carolina seceded.

Suddenly, just months before he was to leave the White House, Buchanan was faced with the biggest crisis of his career. How could he save the Union if South Carolina had seceded and other southern states were threatening to do the same?

Many southerners thought that Buchanan would support secession. After all, he had long been considered a friend of the South, even though he was from a northern state. He spoke fondly of the southern plantation lifestyle. Plantation society, with its traditions and respect for landownership, appealed to him more than northern society with its industries and big cities. From his support of the proslavery Lecompton constitution to his agreement with the Supreme Court's Dred Scott decision, Buchanan had long shown himself to be a friend of the South.

But the president soon made it clear that he did not condone secession. He declared that no state had the right to secede from the Union. He added that Abraham Lincoln had been legally elected and that the South had no right to break up the Union over his election. The American principle of self-government—letting the majority of the people decide the country's course—had to be respected. At the same time, Buchanan said that by condemning slavery, northerners were encroaching on the rights of southerners.

Soon after seceding, South Carolina asked Buchanan to remove Union troops from Fort Sumter, a federal garrison in Charleston Harbor. Buchanan refused and instead sent reinforcements to the fort. But rather than sending a navy ship, which might provoke the South, he sent an unarmed steamer, the *Star of the West*. On January 9, 1861, South Carolina troops fired on the ship, which turned around and headed back to New York. Technically, this was the beginning of the Civil War, because shots had been fired at a U.S. ship. However, Buchanan claimed there had been no act of war, since no one had been injured. Although everyone agreed that war was inevitable, the president seemed determined to hand the country over to Lincoln before fighting began.

LAST CHANCE

Buchanan made one last effort to avoid war. He asked Congress to come up with a proposal to stop more states from seceding. The result was the Crittenden Compromise, named after its author, Senator John Crittenden of Kentucky. Under the proposal, slavery would continue in all states in which it currently existed, as well as in Washington, D.C. The proposal also protected the interstate slave trade (the buying and selling of slaves across state borders) and promised a return to the old dividing line set by the Missouri Compromise of 1820. Slavery would forever be banned north of that line and allowed south of the line.

But neither the North nor the South was satisfied with the terms of this compromise. Southerners felt it did not do enough to protect slave owners. Northerners did not want to allow the spread of slavery into any new territories or states, such as new western states south of the Missouri Compromise dividing line.

With no support for the Crittenden Compromise, Buchanan saw few alternatives to war. In less than one month, from January 9 to February 1, six more states— Mississippi, Florida, Alabama, Georgia, Louisiana, and Texas—left the Union. On February 4, the seven states that had seceded declared themselves to be a new nation, the Confederate States of America.

Critics accused Buchanan of doing nothing to prevent war as the Union fell apart. They claimed he was simply trying to hold off the beginning of the fighting until March 1861, when his term would end. But Buchanan later wrote in his autobiography that he felt he needed to act with caution. He thought that by remaining calm, he could keep the eight other slave states from seceding. He also believed that the seven Confederate states would soon disagree among themselves and return to the Union.

CHAPTER NINE

BACK TO WHEATLAND

*I have always felt and still feel that I
[performed] every public duty imposed on me
conscientiously. I have no regret for any
public act of my life and history
will [defend] my memory.*
—James Buchanan

Buchanan undoubtedly felt a great sense of relief upon leaving the White House. During Lincoln's inauguration, he sat in the Capitol's eastern entrance, just steps from where he himself had taken the oath of office four years earlier. He reflected on his own inaugural speech, during which he had promised to dedicate himself to preserving the Union. He felt satisfied that, given the circumstances, he had done his best to uphold this promise. Although seven states had left the Union, the border slave states (those farthest north) were still part of the United States. He was handing over the presidency to Lincoln without any admission that southern states had the right to secede. And he had successfully kept Union troops in Fort Sumter, despite much protest from South Carolina.

Buchanan stayed in Washington with a friend, Robert Ould, for one night after Lincoln was inaugurated. The next day, he boarded a train to Pennsylvania. He wrote at the time that his plans were only "to perform the duties of a good citizen and a kind friend and neighbor." For one night, he stopped in Baltimore, where he gave two speeches. He was greeted with shouts of "Three cheers for Old Buck" and "Three more for the last president of the *United* States!"—a sarcastic comment on the disintegrating Union.

The next morning, he boarded the same train car that had taken him to his inauguration in 1857 and headed for Lancaster. His hometown welcomed him with a thirty-four-gun presidential salute, a cannon blast, and the ringing of church bells. The townspeople formed a two-mile parade to the town square for speeches, and later, another parade escorted the retired president home to Wheatland.

Buchanan quickly settled into the life of a retired gentleman at Wheatland. His niece and nephew, Harriet and James, had moved home with him from the White House. In his first few months at home, he received many visitors, both old friends he had not seen since he had left for Washington and new friends who had not yet visited Wheatland.

Meanwhile, Buchanan was happy to see that Lincoln was following his general policy. The new president had neither admitted the right of secession by the southern states nor used force against them. But when Confederate forces fired on Fort Sumter on April 12, 1861, Lincoln

Lincoln officially declared war after this southern attack on Fort Sumter.

---◇---

finally declared war. Buchanan noted that Lincoln "had no alternative but to accept the war instigated by South Carolina and the Southern Confederacy." Four years of bloody civil war followed.

CHARACTER ATTACKS

Buchanan may have wished for a peaceful retirement, but it was not to be. Almost as soon as he arrived at Wheatland, vicious rumors began swirling around the country. One newspaper reported that he had used eight thousand dollars in government funds to buy personal furnishings for the White House. Another reported that he and Harriet had stolen valuable paintings from the White House. These rumors proved to be false, but their frequency hurt Buchanan. But what really stung him was the public sentiment underlying the rumors. Many people seemed to believe that he was responsible for the outbreak of the Civil War.

Many northern newspapers called Buchanan a traitor for having been sympathetic to the southern cause during his term in office.

Even the U.S. Senate tried to slander Buchanan's name. Some senators introduced a formal resolution, or statement, condemning him for not preventing southern secession. The resolution did not get enough votes to pass in the Senate, but the damage to Buchanan's reputation was done.

Buchanan was deeply hurt by these accusations, and he tried to defend himself publicly against them. But with the Civil War raging, it seemed that the public had decided to make Buchanan a scapegoat. Every time he tried to defend himself by writing his own newspaper article, his argument was turned against him. Even some former cabinet members refused to defend him against false accusations.

BOOK OF DEFENSE

Buchanan soon realized that he would not be able to defend his character publicly until the Civil War was over. The public was too eager to blame somebody for the situation. Instead, he began collecting all the newspaper articles attacking him and writing his own personal defenses against each attack. He planned to publish a book describing his actions as president in great detail. He wanted to prove to everyone that he had done all he could to prevent war. He finished his first draft in 1862 but did not want to publish it until after the war. Buchanan knew that the public needed to cool down before it would be receptive to his explanations.

In his book, Buchanan carefully documented his actions as president, explaining at each turn why he did what he did.

He wrote that the Civil War was the result of fifty years of anger and violence between the North and the South over slavery. He argued that he and President Lincoln had basically followed the same policies. Both presidents denied that the southern states had any right to secede from the Union. Both faced the same question regarding Fort Sumter—whether to surrender it to South Carolina or to strengthen Union troops there. Buchanan and Lincoln had both decided to reinforce the Union troops rather than give up the fort. It was only after Fort Sumter was attacked that Lincoln had declared war, and Buchanan said that he would have done the same thing. In short, Buchanan argued, he had not been soft on the South and was not responsible for the outbreak of war.

FINAL YEARS

The Civil War ended with a northern victory in April 1865. Buchanan's book, called *Mr. Buchanan's Administration on the Eve of the Rebellion,* was published one year later. With the war's end and the book's publication, Buchanan hoped that the public would begin to change their negative opinions of him. But it didn't happen.

MR. BUCHANAN'S

ADMINISTRATION

ON THE

EVE OF THE REBELLION.

NEW YORK:
D. APPLETON AND COMPANY,
443 & 445 BROADWAY.
1866.

———————————— ✧

Buchanan wrote a book about his presidency in the hope of restoring his reputation.

The attacks on Buchanan's character had cost him many friends in the last years of his life. And many families who lost loved ones in the war held the former president personally responsible for their losses.

Other old friends, however, remained loyal to Buchanan, and in his final years at Wheatland, he often entertained both friends and family. In January 1866, his niece Harriet married Henry E. Johnston, a banker from Baltimore. Harriet moved to Baltimore, but she continued to visit her uncle often. Buchanan also visited her at least once and met her first-born child.

In May 1868, at the age of seventy-eight, Buchanan became very ill with a cold. He began to prepare himself for dying and drew up a new will. He died at home on June 1. After his death, a packet of yellowing letters from his long-ago love Ann was found at Wheatland.

Buchanan had written that he wanted to be buried in Lancaster without any pomp or public ceremony or even a parade. But when he died, his wishes were not followed. More than twenty thousand people attended his funeral at Woodward Hill Cemetery in Lancaster three days later. Speakers described his "private virtues, integrity, charity, kindness, and courtesy." In his will, he left Wheatland to Harriet, who used it as a summer house until the death of her husband in 1884.

Buchanan's final hope was that negative public opinion about him would gradually fade after his death. He felt that he had been unfairly blamed for the bloodshed of the Civil War, and he expected that eventually the facts would clear his name. But historians have not been able to agree on whether Buchanan could have prevented the Civil War or not. Some say that a stronger president could have convinced the North and the South to settle their differences peacefully. Others say that the Civil War was destined to happen no matter what the president did or did not do. And some even say that by refusing to use force against the South, Buchanan prevented the war from beginning earlier or causing more deaths than it did. More than 140 years after his presidency ended, the debate continues.

Remembering James Buchanan

In 1930 sculptor Hans Schuler created a bronze statue of James Buchanan. The statue shows the president seated on a granite platform with one figure on either side of him—one representing law and one representing democracy. The statue stands at Sixteenth and Euclid streets in northwestern Washington, D.C.

The James Buchanan Foundation for the Preservation of Wheatland was formed in 1936. This private, not-for-profit group based in Lancaster owns Wheatland and operates tours of the home. Tour guides lead groups through the mansion and its grounds every day from April through October. Special programs for young people include a hands-on Victorian life tour that explores the transportation, communications, and clothing of Buchanan's day. Another tour allows students to view the mansion through the eyes of a household servant.

✧ ——————————
Buchanan's statue is located in Rock Creek Park, Washington, D.C., along with twenty other monuments, statues, and memorials.

TIMELINE

1791   James Buchanan is born on April 23 in a log cabin near Mercersburg, Pennsylvania.

1797   The Buchanan family moves to Mercersburg, where James's father runs a general store.

1807   James enters Dickinson College in Carlisle, Pennsylvania.

1809   Buchanan graduates from Dickinson College and moves to Lancaster, Pennsylvania, to study law.

1812   Buchanan sets up a law practice in Lancaster.

1814   Buchanan volunteers to fight in the War of 1812. He is elected to the Pennsylvania legislature as a member of the Federalist Party.

1815   Buchanan is reelected to a second term in the Pennsylvania legislature.

1816   Buchanan returns to Lancaster to practice law.

1818   Buchanan meets Ann Coleman and falls in love.

1819   James and Ann become engaged. Ann dies in December.

1820   Buchanan is elected to the U.S. Congress.

1821   Buchanan begins his term in Congress.

1824   Buchanan supports Andrew Jackson, the Democratic Party candidate for U.S. president. John Quincy Adams defeats Jackson.

1828   Buchanan again supports Jackson's candidacy for president. Jackson is elected president in November.

1831   President Jackson appoints Buchanan U.S. minister to Russia.

1832 As minister to Russia, Buchanan negotiates the first trade treaty between the United States and Russia.

1834 Buchanan is elected to the U.S. Senate as a Democrat. He serves in the Senate for ten years.

1845 President James Polk appoints Buchanan secretary of state.

1849 Zachary Taylor of the Whig Party is inaugurated as president. Buchanan returns to Lancaster.

1853 Franklin Pierce of the Democratic Party is inaugurated as president. He appoints Buchanan minister to Great Britain.

1856 Buchanan is elected president of the United States as a Democrat.

1860 Republican Abraham Lincoln is elected president in November. South Carolina secedes from the Union in December.

1861 Abraham Lincoln is sworn in as president in March. The Civil War officially starts in April when southern troops fire on Fort Sumter, South Carolina.

1866 Buchanan's book, *Mr. Buchanan's Administration on the Eve of the Rebellion,* is published.

1868 Buchanan dies on June 1 at Wheatland.

Source Notes

7 Philip S. Klein, *President James Buchanan: A Biography* (University Park: Pennsylvania State University Press, 1962), 402.

8 Ibid.

10 Ibid., xviii.

16 Ibid., 8.

16 Ibid., 9.

18 Ibid., 10.

21 Ibid., 24.

30 Ibid., 32.

30 Ibid., 33.

31 Ibid., 40.

40 Frederick Moore Binder, *James Buchanan and the American Empire* (Selinsgrove, PA: Susquehanna University Press, 1994), 36.

41 Klein, *President James Buchanan,* 147.

50 Binder, *James Buchanan,* 51.

53 Klein, *President James Buchanan,* 192.

58 Ibid., 207.

58 Ibid.

61 Binder, *James Buchanan,* 172.

61 Ibid., 173.

61 Ibid., 175.

61 Ibid.

62 Ibid.

64 Klein, *President James Buchanan,* 243.

67 Ibid., 194.

68 Ibid., 252.

72 Elbert B. Smith, *The Presidency of James Buchanan* (Lawrence: University Press of Kansas, 1975), 6.

73 Klein, *President James Buchanan,* 257.

74 Ibid., 260.

77 Ibid., 300.

79 Irving J. Sloan, ed., *James Buchanan, 1791–1868* (Dobbs Ferry, NY: Oceana Publications, 1968), 21.

79 Ibid., 22.

79 Klein, *President James Buchanan,* 272.

81 Ibid., 275.

89 Ibid., 337.

97 Klein, *President James Buchanan,* 428.

98 Bruce Catton, *The Coming Fury* (New York: Doubleday and Co., 1961), 263.

99 Klein, *President James Buchanan,* 374.

102 Ibid., 428.

BIBLIOGRAPHY

Binder, Frederick Moore. *James Buchanan and the American Empire.* Selinsgrove, PA: Susquehanna University Press, 1994.

Birkner, Michael J., ed. *James Buchanan and the Political Crisis of the 1850s.* Selinsgrove, PA: Susquehanna University Press, 1996.

Buchanan, James. *Mr. Buchanan's Administration on the Eve of the Rebellion.* New York: Appleton and Company, 1866. Reprint, Scituate, MA: Digital Scanning Inc., 2000.

Catton, Bruce. *The Coming Fury.* New York: Doubleday and Co., 1961.

Klein, Philip S. *President James Buchanan: A Biography.* University Park: Pennsylvania State University Press, 1962.

Sloan, Irving J., ed. *James Buchanan, 1791–1868.* Dobbs Ferry, NY: Oceana Publications, 1968.

Smith, Elbert B. *The Presidency of James Buchanan.* Lawrence: University Press of Kansas, 1975.

FURTHER READING AND WEBSITES

Arnold, James R., *The Civil War.* Minneapolis: Lerner Publications Company, 2005.

Behrman, Carol H., *Andrew Jackson.* Minneapolis: Lerner Publications Company, 2003.

———. *James K. Polk.* Minneapolis: Lerner Publications Company, 2005.

Childress, Diana. *The War of 1812.* Minneapolis: Lerner Publications Company, 2004.

Naden, Corinne J., and Rose Blue. *Why Fight? The Causes of the American Civil War.* Austin, TX: Steck-Vaughn Company, 2000.

Nelson, Vaunda Micheaux. *Almost to Freedom.* Minneapolis: Carolrhoda Books, 2004.

Shelley, Mary V. *Harriet Lane: First Lady of the White House.* New York: Sutter House, 1980.

Suffolk Web: Just Curious about the Civil War
  http://www.suffolk.lib.ny.us/youth/jccivil.html
  This website for kids offers links to more than two dozen other Civil War websites, including sites addressing causes of the war, women in the war, battles, war photos, and much more.

Swain, Gwenyth. *Pennsylvania.* Minneapolis: Lerner Publications Company, 2002.

Take a Look at Wheatland
  http://www.lanccounty.com/wheatland/
  This website offers information on and pictures of Buchanan's estate, Wheatland, as well as biographical information on James Buchanan and Harriet Lane.

White House Biography of James Buchanan
  http://www.whitehouse.gov/history/presidents/jb15.html
  This website features a brief biography of President Buchanan.

World Almanac for Kids' Biography of James Buchanan
  http://www.worldalmanacforkids.com/explore/presidents
  /buchanan_james.html
  This website features a short biography of President Buchanan, as well as links to related people and events.

Worth, Richard. *Westward Expansion and Manifest Destiny in American History.* New York: Enslow Publishers, 2001.

Young, Jeff C. *James Buchanan.* Berkeley Heights, NJ: Enslow Publishers, 2003.

INDEX

ABOUT THE AUTHOR

Sandy Donovan has written many books for young readers, on topics including history, civics, and biology. Donovan has also worked as a newspaper reporter and a magazine editor, and she holds a bachelor's degree in journalism and a master's degree in public policy. She has lived and traveled in Europe, Asia, and the Middle East. She lives in Minneapolis, Minnesota, with her husband and sons. Donovan's titles include *Making Laws: A Look at How a Bill Becomes a Law*, *Protecting America: A Look at the People Who Keep Our Country Safe*, and *The Channel Tunnel*.
